# Faith
## ACTIVATED

# *Faith*

## ACTIVATED

· · · · · · · · ·

*A 90 day journal experience designed to help you activate*

*your faith and transform your dreams into reality.*

*with* RACHEL LUNA

# Table *of* Contents

## PROMPTS

# Introduction

We've all been mislead, and unfortunately, to peak your interest, I've kept up with the pretense. But now that I've got your attention, I can tell you the truth.

This isn't really a journal. If you look up the definition of journal in the dictionary you'll find this:

> **jour·nal**
>
> jərnl/
>
> *noun*
>
> a newspaper or magazine that deals with a particular subject or professional activity.
>
> a daily record of news and events of a personal nature; a diary.

This book is *neither* of those things and the process I'm going to show you in the upcoming pages have nothing to do with you keeping a record of events or launching a newspaper or magazine.

Rather, I'm going to show you how to use a sheet of paper to script the life of your dreams and manifest your desires with ease, energy, and excitement.

**REAL TALK: I wasn't always a believer in this whole "journaling to manifest" thing.**

For years I'd heard stories from people who swore journaling and keeping vision boards was the secret to their success. But honestly, I didn't believe it. After all, I had been keeping diaries and journals all my life with little to show for it. I was faithful to record my daily comings and goings. I would even write my goals and action plans with loving care and attention. But those activities didn't really seem to be moving the needle forward.

Then I discovered the critical difference between keeping a diary and journaling with the intention to manifest your dreams.

**KEEPING A RECORD OF YOUR DAY TO DAY ACTIVITY ISN'T GOING TO HELP YOU MANIFEST WHAT YOU DESIRE.**

Keeping a log of your daily activities isn't a bad thing. Heck, it's great if you plan on writing a memoir one day. But it doesn't do much to help you propel your life forward and generate the results you crave. The only real way to make that happen is to:

1. Ask and answer powerful questions to uncover the limiting beliefs that have been holding you back.

2. Script your life as you wish it to be, as if it already were (I'll break that down in the upcoming pages).

3. Stay committed to making this a daily practice.

Three seemingly simple steps that so many people avoid, resist and take for granted. But I know, both from my own experience and from having coached and supported hundreds of members inside my Faith Activated Journing Experience Membership that doing these 3 steps consistently yield amazing breakthroughs and results.

Results like:

April Kamara Rachel.... This course is worth MILLIONS.

You are giving your ALL, and I feel like i paid PENNIES in comparison to the value this course holds.

Thank you for this! THANK YOU SO MUCH!

Love · Reply · 33w

 1

Alyssa Jenkins Omg this prompt is gold! I found out that my sense of perfectionism was keeping me from pursuing avenues of income that I've been thinking about for a long time but have been too scared actually enact. No more! If I make mistakes, I'll just learn from them, and I'll adjust! I discovered some other stuff too, but I think this was the biggest take away

Love · Reply · 24w

 2

**Kendra Hennessy**
August 2 at 1:06 PM · 🏷 Add Topics          •••

On Tuesday, I ended my journal entry with "This launch feels like the best ever. It feels right. It feels aligned. It feels like I'm giving in the perfect amount." followed by gratitude and praise.

Today, my ad manager called me to say that this ad campaign is our best ever, with results so good, she's shocked!

Write it into existence and lead with faith!!

And now you have the opportunity to enjoy the same - if not, better - results.  So grab your favorite writing tool (mine happens to be PaperMate™ InkJoy Gel 0.7 pens), a cup of whatever makes you feel nurtured, comfortable, and at ease, (I love hot coffee or mint tea) and let's begin.

P.S. If, as you're going through the journal, you discover you'd like additional support, access to secret images of my personal journal entries, coaching support or simply a community to go through this experience with, I personally invite you to join us inside The Faith Activated Journaling Experience.  You can learn more by visiting www.RachelLuna.biz/faith

All my love,

Rachel

# WRITE THE

*vision*,

## MAKE IT PLAIN

Habakkuk 2:2

# About the Author

**THE HIGHLIGHTS:**

I'm Rachel Luna, best selling author of the book, Successful People are Full of C.R.A.P. (Courage. Resilience. Authenticity. Perseverance): A Step-by-Step Guide to Getting it Together & Achieving Your Dreams, speaker, + Chief Confidence Creator here at RachelLuna.Biz.

I help remarkable individuals just like you get clear, confident and taking consistent action, so you can do that big thing you were born to do. I've helped thousands of people around the world through my book, weekly emails, speaking tours, workshops and digital courses.

I've been invited to speak all around the globe from Good Morning America's Tory Johnson Spark & Hustle tour and Princeton University to as far away as Germany and Japan! I've also been featured in Forbes, Latina Magazine, Success Magazine and am a Huffington Post contributor.

**FUN FACTS ABOUT MOI**

Just a few lil' things I thought you might like to know...

- I've moved more than 17 times in the last 10 years and at the time this journal went to print we had just finished purchasing our first dream house. This house has everything I journaled about having 4 years prior to when we bought it. **#faithactivatedjournalingworks**

- I love to travel and have been to over 18 countries, even though I used to be

**afraid of flying.** Lesson of the day: Never let your fears stop you from achieving your dreams! The more you face your fears, the quicker you'll overcome them. (I still get a little nervous when it's turbulent)

- **I have two tattoos.** One on my right forearm that says, "And I will listen." (from the bible verse Jeremiah 29:12) And one on my leg that says "U.S.M.C. Decisions Determine Destiny" - oh, I'm a former US Marine who served 10 yrs and am an Iraqi War Vet.

- **I have clocked in over 10,000 hours of 1:1 coaching** over the last 9 years - that's a lot of sessions! Hey, I guess that makes me an expert! ;-)

- Chocolate. **I love chocolate.**

If you're like me and want to know even more, here's the

## LONG STORY...

My life shouldn't be as amazing as it is today...

## AT LEAST NOT ACCORDING TO STATISTICS...

My parents both died of AIDS, my brothers, sisters, and I were all split up. Truth be told, decades passed without me even knowing where a few of them were.

Two eating disorders in my early teens, a battle with severe depression, a stint in AA, and some other less than brilliant choices all could have made me yet another stat.

But, as a Christian woman, I've always known that God purposed me to do, be and achieve more than I was giving myself credit for. There were days when I would stand in awe of my gorgeous family, adventurous lifestyle & financial freedom, wondering — how did I get here?

## GROWING UP IN THE CONCRETE JUNGLE OF NYC...

I dreamt of twinkling lights, red carpets and crystal-clinking galas. I thought I was destined for fame. But a conversation at Footlocker changed everything.

I was 16 when a co-worker said she was joining the Marine Corps. Even though I was 4'11, suffered from activity induced asthma and was athletically challenged (I was the girl who made excuses to get out of gym class), I wanted in!

*As crazy as it sounds, I wanted to prove to myself I could do it.* I also wanted to find a way to learn how to be a fit and healthy person and end my eating troubles once and for all. At 19, I enlisted in the Reserves, lost 18lbs and became a half-marathon runner.

Four years later, I was deployed to Iraq. After returning to the U.S., my journey took me from the audition rooms of LA (where I kept forgetting my lines) to scraping by on waitress tips to the prestigious boardrooms of Goldman Sachs. I found corporate America dull and Hollywood egocentric, so I went running back to my beloved Corps.

Eighteen countries & four languages(ish) later, I was still trying to figure out what I wanted to do with my life!

## LIFE'S TOO SHORT...

In 2006, I was stationed as a caregiver for wounded warriors at a hospital in Germany — it changed EVERYTHING. Here I came to know men with missing limbs, gruesome burns and other life-altering conditions. Their positive determination to rebuild their lives forever changed my outlook — life's too short to continue living other people's dreams.

I knew I wanted to combine my love of performance with my desire to change lives, but wasn't sure how to do it. I also had a lot of debt (over $40,000 to be precise), failed relationships and plain ole fear weighing me down.

So, I made a few changes.

I began journaling over the things I wanted.

I invested in myself and hired a life coach to help me work through the sludge.

I took my life and my dreams seriously — and it paid off!

Within ONE year (I kid you not) I got completely out of debt, ran my very first ½ marathon (and kicked my eating disorders for good!) met & married the man of my dreams and clarified my calling:

helping others find the clarity and confidence they need to step into their full purpose and gain financial freedom doing those *BIG THINGS* they were meant to do.

I don't tell you this to brag — today my life is far from perfect — but rather to **invite you to do the same!**

*YOU can live your dreams, have an amazing business, financial independence and blessed relationships, too!*

With this journal, I hope to help you take the first steps towards achieving your dreams and more!  Let's get to work.

xoxo,

Rachel

# REHEARSE THE TRUTH

# UNTIL IT BECOMES

## *reality*

Dr. Faith Wokoma

# *Resisting Resistance*

Resistance is the refusal to accept or comply with something. The first thing I want you to do the moment you feel resistance around journaling is to ask yourself the following questions,

*"Why am I refusing to accept that journaling is what I should be doing right now?"*

*"Why am I refusing to accept that when I journal, I will be able to manifest my desires?"*

*"Is there a belief around journaling and manifesting that I need to work on?"*

You are now embarking on an experiment and you will have to challenge yourself to answer the tough questions.

A word of caution: **"I don't know"** is never an acceptable answer. *"I don't know"* is what we say when we haven't taken the time to search for the answers or when the answer is so terrifying we can't even admit it to ourselves, let alone share it with others. If your answer is, *"I don't know"* please do not settle for that. Press on because a breakthrough is near.

Back to resistance. Resistance often shows up just as you're about to do something that will challenge you, stretch you or lead you to growth. It's not uncommon for people to begin a journal practice and be met with resistance and ultimately decide, *"It's not working for me."*

I encourage you to keep reading as I help you resist resistance. I remind you that like any practice, this may take time to develop.

When it comes to resistance, we typically resist the things we want most, or the things that will bring about the biggest change and growth in our lives.

**Why do we resist the things we say we want?**

I go into a lot more detail inside the Faith Activated Journaling Experience, but here's the quick answer -

We resist the things we say we want because we are experiencing cognitive dissonance. In plain terms, we resist the things we say we want because we are INDECISIVE and have inconsistent and conflicting inner thoughts.

The great news is that there are simple practices you can implement to resist resistance. Here's a snapshot of what to do whenever you face resistance both in your journaling practice and in life.

1. **Ask yourself, "What is the first step?" I need to take today to manifest my dreams and desires.**

   Understand that you do not need to know the entire journey to start manifesting your dreams. Nor do you need to know "how" it's going to happen. I see a lot of people struggle with manifesting because they are focused on how it's going to happen rather than simply asking, "What is my first step right now?"

2. **Check in with your Identity.**

   Examine who you wish to be and who you are currently being. How would you act and behave if you already had everything you've ever wanted? What would your journal entries look like? How would you show up to your journal practice? How would you approach your daily actions?

   The identity of the person who has what you're trying to manifest would behave differently than how you're behaving right now and they would approach resistance differently.  Ask yourself, how would future me handle this resistance?  Then move into action as your future self.

3.  **Give yourself grace.**

    If you're new to journaling, give yourself an extra dose of grace.  New habits take time and practice.  When you feel resistance coming in, acknowledge it, apply the steps above and then give yourself grace to grow into this new practice.  You'll start to see the shifts if you're open to seeing them with love, compassion and grace for yourself.

Now that you have the basics down, it's time to start journaling!  I'm so excited for all you will manifest as a result of being consistent with this practice.  I'd love to hear from you.  Please email me: faith@rachelluna.biz and share your breakthroughs, aha moments and testimonials.  I can't wait to hear from you.

xoxo,

Rachel

YOUR GIFT IS IN
HELPING OTHERS IN
THE AREAS YOU'VE

CJ Quinney

# Mindset & Beliefs

"Once your mindset changes, everything on the outside
will change along with it." - Steve Maraboli

*What 1 action, if taken today and completed to my best ability, will allow me to feel like I've won?*

*Who would I need to be if I were to receive all of the personal and financial growth I desire?*

*Today I am...*

*How will I make today an amazing experience for myself, my business and my loved ones?*

*How do I wish to FEEL as I go through this day?*

*My favorite moments of the day are when I...*

*What if I committed to starting and following through all the way to the end of this journaling experience?*

*What would it mean for me to play a bigger game?*

*How have I stopped myself from showing up at my fullest potential?*

*Today I am committed to...*

*When I think of my success I feel...*

*When I think of my failures or possible future failure, I'm afraid...*
*These fears are irrational because...*

*Today I choose and accept...*

*I believe time is...*

*What is the story/narrative/belief that has guided my actions, decisions and life?*

*What have I (am I continuing to) denied/deny myself as a result of living my story/belief?*

*Why can't I have the things and life I say I want?*

*Why are the things and life I say I want ABSOLUTELY possible for me?*

*If the way I leave this month is the way I will enter next month, what will I leave behind? What will I allow to come with me into the new month?*

*On a scale of 1-10, 1 being not my best, 10 being my absolute best, how did I show up for myself this week?*

*This week I am so happy that...*

*This month I earned... (insert your financial goal as if it were already true)*

*I achieved this financial goal because I was...*

*If this were a month of TOTAL alignment, my days would be ...*

# WOW! I amazed myself when I ...

*(Insert how you ended this month and how you began the first day of the upcoming month)*

*My biggest fear heading into the new month is.... And I'm excited that I did it anyway because...*

*My most memorable moment of this month was (use this prompt to script the upcoming month)...*

*Journaling has allowed me to...*

*Envision. Create. Activate.*

*Envision. Create. Activate.*

*Envision. Create. Activate.*

# *Habits*

*"Depending on what they are, our habits will either make us or break us.*

*We become what we repeatedly do." - Sean Covey*

*I'm so grateful for everything I already have. What I currently do not have, but want in my life is...*

*The habits that are currently serving me are _____. The habits that are currently NOT serving me and need to be replaced or modified are _____.*

*(Identity level) My current identity around the habits that are NOT serving me is someone who is _____.*

*(Belief level) My current belief around the habits that are NOT serving me is that _____.*

*(Self Talk) The things I tell myself and others around the habits I want to change is that _____.*

*(Behavior) The behaviors I take when practicing unhealthy habits are*

————————————.

*I am excited to take on new identities, beliefs, self-talk and behaviors in the following areas*

_____. *This month I am working on (pick ONE habit to focus on changing/modifying/*

*breaking/creating)* _____.

# REFLECTION

# REFLECTION

# REFLECTION

# REFLECTION

# REFLECTION

# REFLECTION

*At the beginning of the month my identity was ... Today I am choosing my identity to be ...*

*Showing up each day, BEING the person I desire to identify with most, I've been able to ...*

*The new habit I've enjoyed shifting into has been _____, because ...*

*I've found myself struggling to embody my true/desired identity when ...*
*When this happens I ...*

*My beliefs at the beginning of the month were... Some beliefs have shifted and now I believe ...*

*This month, my self talk has been (positive, neutral, negative). I find myself telling myself....*

*Today I am choosing neutral and/or positive self talk statements. When it comes to being able to achieve my goals and dreams, I am telling myself ...*

*The habit I am working on shifting this week is _____. My current identity around this is _____. My current belief(s) is/are that _____. My self talk about this habit has been ...*

*Today, as I shift my habit, the identity I am taking on means I am ... (Make list of "I Am" statements of who you have to be)*

*My new self talk around the habit I am focusing on this week is ...*

*The behaviors I act on this week as a result of my new identity, belief and self talk have been/will be to ... (list the actions/behaviors for this habit)*

*Working on the habit I've wanted to shift this week has allowed me to grow as a person because...*

*Today I get to be someone who...*

*Today, the actions I take are instigated by someone who believes ...*

*Each day I remind myself that I am ... (insert your true/desired identity) and this allows me to show up and (insert the behaviors of your true/desired identity)*

*I've loved myself most this month when I ...*

*Moving forward, I get to be someone who ...*

*When others make comments about the changes I've made (positive or negative) I am now able to feel confident because my true/desired identity is one of someone who would respond to them by ... (insert how you desire to handle positive and negative feedback)*

Envision. Create. Activate.

Envision. Create. Activate.

*Envision. Create. Activate.*

# *Money*

"*Money is a tool. It will take you where you wish, but it will not replace you as the driver.*" - Ayn Rand

*Today I am claiming $_____ and am releasing my emotional attachment to how I will receive it. I am activating my faith and trusting it is already mine.  Knowing that I don't have to worry about how this money is arriving into my account makes me feel...*

*I believe money is...*

*What does money mean to me?*

*Respecting money means...*

*Money Date: Look at your finances then journal - When I saw my true financial situation I felt... I am now changing and upleveling my financial situation and reality by...*

*How have I been blocking my ability to receive/earn/keep money? Dig Deeper: Why am I resisting money?*
*(i.e. it doesn't feel like real money. I didn't work for it. It seems like an extra time hassle for "just $20")*

*In the past, I have been _____ with my money.  Being this way has made me feel _____. (ex.*
*In the past I have been irresponsible with my money.  Being this way has made me feel fearful that I will be*
*irresponsible in the future)*

*I forgive myself (and anyone else) for... (make a list of at least 15 people, circumstances, events that you associate with money or guilt to forgive) (i.e. I forgive my mom for telling me that how bills were paid was none of my business. This moment in my life led me to ...The lesson I learned was...)*

*If my faith around money were increased, then I'd feel... (i.e. less anxious, abundant, at ease, I'd pray more prayers of praise for what's already received even if I can't see it, etc)*

*If I had an extra $_____ per month I would feel... With that money I would _____.*

*How much money would I need to feel "financially free?" If I were financially free, my ideal day would be ...*

*The reasons I can't have the money I desire are... (list at least 5 reasons why you believe you can't be financially free). Dig deeper: Rewrite all the reasons you can and will be financially free.*

*When it comes to money, I'm really confident that ...*

*What it comes to money, I need to learn more about _____ so that I can _____. Having this financial literacy will help me...*

*How would I manage things differently if I had all the money I desire?*

*Today I am grateful for...*

*I'm so excited about the money I am receiving because with it, I will...*

*"Faith without works is dead." The actions I can and will take to activate my faith around money are...*

*My new money beliefs are... (create 10 - 15 money affirmations that make you feel really empowered around money)*

*I feel the most resistance around money when...*

*I sometimes feel guilty around money because...*

*If I had the money I desire then others around me would...*

*I'm excited to celebrate my financial freedom by...*

*I struggle to spend money on _____ because I feel... I enjoy spending money on ...*

*Celebrate, thank, appreciate and honor the people in your life who contribute to your financial freedom. Who are you thanking and why?*

*I am grateful for any debt (past or present) because it gave/taught me...*

*Gratitude Rampage - Write 25-50 things you're grateful for right in this moment.*

*Envision. Create. Activate.*

*Envision. Create. Activate.*

Envision. Create. Activate.

Free Space

Envision. Create. Activate.

*Envision. Create. Activate.*

Envision. Create. Activate.

*Envision. Create. Activate.*

Envision. Create. Activate.

*Envision. Create. Activate.*

*Envision. Create. Activate.*

*Envision. Create. Activate.*

*Envision. Create. Activate.*

*Envision. Create. Activate.*

*Envision. Create. Activate.*

*Envision. Create. Activate.*

# BEHOLD, I HAVE GIVEN YOU

*authority* ...

Luke 10:19

# *This is Only the Beginning*

Hello beautiful.  You may have completed the Faith Activated Journal, but this isn't the end - it's only the beginning.

I'd love to continue to support you, whether in life or business, I'm here for you.  To learn more about manifesting, journaling and entrepreneurship, visit me at: www.RachelLuna.biz

When you get there you'll find tons of free resources - downloads, workbooks, planner sheets, audios, and even a free chapter of my latest book, Girl, Confident.

Want to take it to the next level and work with me?  Awesome! You can get all the details by going to www.RachelLuna.biz/work

If you're into podcasts, I invite you to subscribe to my show, Real Talk with Rachel Luna. It's available on iTunes, Stitcher, Google Play, iHeart Radio, and Spotify.  It's packed full of content designed to help you gain more clarity, confidence and gain a real inside look behind the scenes of successful businesses.

And finally, for daily entertainment and real strategy, follow me on Instagram @GirlConfident.

I can't wait to hear your amazing testimonials, so don't forget to email me at faith@rachelluna.biz

All my love,

Rachel